The Big Bible Prayer Book

First published 2017
ISBN 978 1 78506 558 3

Scripture Union, Trinity House, Opal Court, Opal Drive,
Fox Milne, Milton Keynes, MK15 0DF, UK
Email: info@scriptureunion.org.uk
Website: www.scriptureunion.org.uk

British Library Cataloguing-in-Publication Data. A catalogue record of this book is available from the British Library.

Printed and bound in India by Nutech Print Services - India

Text: Gemma Willis
Design: Luther Spicer
Bible Friends: Mark and Anna Carpenter
Photography: David Vary

Scripture Union is an international Christian charity working with churches in more than 130 countries.

Thank you for purchasing this book. Any profits from this book support SU in England and Wales to bring the good news of Jesus Christ to children, young people and families and to enable them to meet God through the Bible and prayer.

Find out more about our work and how you can get involved at:
www.scriptureunion.org.uk (England and Wales)
www.suscotland.org.uk (Scotland)
www.suni.co.uk (Northern Ireland)
www.scriptureunion.org (USA)
www.su.org.au (Australia)

Thank-you prayers

Help me prayers

Help others prayers

A creation prayer

The sun is yellow in the sky
It shines each day before my eyes
It keeps me warm, it makes things grow
It helps me see which way to go
Thank you, God, for sunny days
Thank you, God, for making ways
For me to see the lovely sun –
Enjoying it is so much fun!

"In the beginning God created the heavens and the earth."

Genesis 1:1

Thank-you prayers

Thank-you prayers

"You take care of the earth and send rain to help the soil grow all kinds of crops.
Your rivers never run dry, and you prepare the earth to produce much grain."

Psalm 65:9

Rainy days

Pitter, patter on the glass
The rain is wet and comes so fast
Rainy days, they help plants grow
Rainy days, they're fun – I know
It falls from clouds up in the air
Big drops, small drops, everywhere
Splashy puddles, drips and drops
Thank you, God, for rain – a lot!

A family prayer

All families are different
They come in different shapes
Some are big and some are small
But all are just as great
Mum, Dad, Sister, Brother
Uncle, Auntie, Old Grandmother!
Thank you, God, for family
Thank you, God, for loving me.

"I will comfort you there like a mother comforting her child."

Isaiah 66:13

Thank-you prayers

Dogs and cats, pigs and sheep

Dogs and cats, pigs and sheep
Woof and miaow, oink and bleet
Lions, zebras, bears and snails
Stompy feet, big teeth, long tails
Thank you, God – they're all so great!
You made them all – I just can't wait
To see some more of all you've done
Thank you, God, for animal fun!

"So the Lord took some soil and made animals and birds. He brought them to the man to see what names he would give each of them. Then the man named the tame animals and the birds and the wild animals."

Genesis 2:19

I love my friends

Thank you, God, for all my friends
They are special to me
They play with me and share my toys
They sometimes come to tea
Thank you, God, for all my friends
They keep me company
But most of all I thank you, God, that
You're a friend to me!

"Servants don't know what their master is doing, and so I don't speak to you as my servants. I speak to you as my friends, and I have told you everything that my Father has told me."

John 15:15

Thank-you prayers

"I pray that God will take care of all your needs with the wonderful blessings that come from Christ Jesus!"

Philippians 4:19

Thank you for yummy food

Beans on toast and yoghurt pots
Tasty chocolate mousse
Thank you, God, for yummy food
Drinks and snacks and juice
Thank you, God, for feeding me
With food that helps me grow
Thank you, God, for all I eat
I'm full from top to toe!

God loves me!

Thank you, God, for loving me
I'm so happy that you do
It's good to know you're always there
Standing with me too
I know I'm sometimes naughty
And sometimes get things wrong
But you'll always love me anyway
And with you I belong
There's nothing I could ever do
To make you love me less
So thank you, God, for loving me
Even when I make a mess!

Thank-you prayers

"God loved the people of this world so much that he gave his only Son, so that everyone who has faith in him will have eternal life and never really die."

John 3:16

I love fun!

I love to play
I love to run
I love to dance
I just love fun
Thank you, God, for smiles and grins
Thank you, God, for games and things
Thank you, God, for making play
Thank you, God, for fun today!

"Come to worship him with thankful hearts and songs of praise."

Psalm 95:2

Just as I am

Just as I am, God made me
Hairy bits, wonky bits
Pointy bits, smooth bits
Thank you, God, for making me.

Just as I am, God made me
Squidgy bits, wiggly bits
Bendy bits, bony bits
Thank you, God, for making me.

Just as I am, God made me
Tiny bits, wobbly bits
All bits, every single one
Thank you, God, for making me.

"But the Lord told him, 'Samuel, don't think Eliab is the one just because he's tall and handsome. He isn't the one I've chosen. People judge others by what they look like, but I judge people by what is in their hearts.'"

1 Samuel 16:7

A prayer for quiet times

Sometimes I am quiet
Sometimes I hide away
But you are always there, God,
You're with me every day.

I like it when it's quiet
It makes me feel OK
I know you understand me
In my own special way.

I know some people find it hard
To see the real me
But you always can, all the time
Right inside you see.

Thank you, God, for quiet
Thank you for being still
Thank you, God, for seeing me
I know you always will.

"Everyone, be silent! The Lord is present and moving about in his holy place."

Zechariah 2:13

Thank you for everyone!

"Whatever you say or do should be done in the name of the Lord Jesus,
as you give thanks to God the Father because of him."

Colossians 3:17

So many people look after me
They make sure I'm right, you see
Grown-ups help to make me grow
There are so many things they know!
Parents, they are always there
Hairdressers will cut my hair
Dentists, they look at my teeth
Inside out and underneath
Doctors check that I'm OK
Teachers teach me every day
Without them I'd have no fun
Thank you, God, for everyone!

Bad dreams

Sometimes when I go to bed
Nasty things get in my head
They make me sad and make me cry
They frighten me, I don't know why.
God, please help me when I sleep
To have good dreams and rest so deep
That when I wake and face the day
Those nasty things have gone away.
You are good and always win
Against every nasty thing
Be with me when I'm in bed and
Put good things into my head.

Help me prayers

" I've commanded you to be strong and brave. Don't ever be afraid or discouraged!
I am the Lord your God, and I will be there to help you wherever you go."

Joshua 1:9

When I am poorly...

I don't like it when I'm sick
It makes me sad and sleepy
Sometimes if I don't get well
I end up weak and weepy
God, please help me when I'm ill
To trust that you are there
Help me to feel better now
With all your loving care.

"You, Lord God, bless everyone who cares for the poor, and you rescue those people in times of trouble. You protect them and keep them alive. You make them happy here in this land, and you don't hand them over to their enemies. You always heal them and restore their strength when they are sick."

Psalm 41:1–3

If I forget you love me

It's lovely that you love me, God,
I'm very glad you do
Help me if I do forget
To show I love you too
When I'm with friends
When I'm at home
Wherever I may be
Help me, God, remember that
You always will love me!

"Love is kind and patient, never jealous, boastful, proud, or rude. Love isn't selfish or quick tempered. It doesn't keep a record of wrongs that others do. Love rejoices in the truth, but not in evil. Love is always supportive, loyal, hopeful, and trusting."

1 Corinthians 13:4—7

Help me prayers

When I am afraid

Sometimes things are scary
They make me feel like jelly
Wibble, wobble, all a-shake
With wiggles in my belly
Scary noises, crawly things
Things I cannot see
Help me, God, be strong and brave
And know you are with me.

"God is our mighty fortress, always ready to help in times of trouble. And so, we won't be afraid!"

Psalm 46:1–2a

Help me to Share

"It's mine," I said, "Not yours," I said
"I don't want to share it!"
"Why can't I just have it all
For me, just mine, no spare bit?!"
When I'm mean, please help me, God,
Remember what you say
That even though it's sometimes hard
Sharing is your way
Help me see it's not all mine
Others can play too
In fact it's better when I share
It's what you say to do.

"But don't forget to help others and to share your possessions with them. This too is like offering a sacrifice that pleases God."

Hebrews 13:16

Loving one another

When people are nice, it's easy to love them
When people are mean, it's not
When they are rude, or bad or cruel
That's when I need a spot
Of your special love and kindness
Your eyes to help me see
How much they mean to you, God,
Even when they're mean to me.

"But I am giving you a new command. You must love each other, just as I have loved you."

John 13:34

But help me, God, to know what's right
And when things aren't OK
Help me, God, to ask for help
From grown-ups who can say
What you would want, what you would do
To make things right again
Help me to love everyone
No matter where or when!

A prayer for sad times

When I'm sad I sometimes cry
When I'm sad it's hard to try
To smile and make a happy face
If I'm in a gloomy place
But I know you're with me God
Giving me a cuddle
Wiping all my tears away
Before they make a puddle!

"You have kept record of my days of wandering. You have stored my tears in your bottle and counted each of them."

Psalm 56:8

It's not fair!

It's hard when things don't go my way
It seems unfair to me
It makes me grumpy all the day
I don't know what to do
Help me, God, to realise
That my ways aren't always best
Remind me that your ways are good
And better than all the rest
Help me to trust you, God,
When I don't get my way.

"I trust your love, and I feel like celebrating because you rescued me."

Psalm 13:5

When I get it wrong

Some days I get it wrong
Sometimes I make a mess
Sometimes I am nasty
And I do not try my best
Sometimes I don't love you, God,
Sometimes I forget
To do what you would want me to
To think before I let
Mean things out or bad things in
I don't always get things right
I'm sorry, God; forgive me, God,
I pray to you this night.

"Instead, be kind and merciful, and forgive others, just as God forgave you because of Christ."

Ephesians 4:32

Jesus, I am sorry

"But if we confess our sins to God, he can always be trusted to forgive us and take our sins away."

1 John 1:9

Jesus, I am sorry
For being mean
For being selfish
For being not like you.

Jesus, I am sorry
For telling lies
For being greedy
For being not like you.

Thank you, Jesus,
That you always, always, always, always, always
Forgive me when I'm sorry
Help me to be more like you.

My friend is sad

Tell Jesus about anyone you know who is sad, and ask him to help.

Jesus, my friend .... is feeling sad because ....

Please will you help them to feel better.

Please will you help me to know how I can help them, too.

Amen.

"Trust God, my friends, and always tell him each one of your concerns. God is our place of safety."

Psalm 62:8

My friend is not very well

Tell Jesus about anyone you know who is unwell, and ask him to help.

Jesus, my friend ....
is not very well.

Please will you make them better.

Please will you help them
to feel calm and safe.

Please will you put caring people
around them who can help.

Amen.

"Jesus went to every town and village. He taught in their meeting places and preached the good news about God's kingdom. Jesus also healed every kind of disease and sickness."

Matthew 9:35

Jesus, please help

Jesus, please, please come and help
When there's not enough
When people don't have what they need
To stay warm, to drink and feed
Themselves and all their family
Jesus, help us all to see
That you tell us we should share and give
All we can to help us live
Together with all that we need
So we all can have enough.

"I look to the hills! Where will I find help? It will come from the Lord, who created the heavens and the earth."

Psalm 121:1–2

Help others prayers

You are always there

I don't like being lonely, God,
I don't think anyone does
It's just not fun to be just me
With no big cuddles and hugs
Jesus, please help lonely people
To know that you are there
And help me know what I can do
To let them know I care.

"You are with me, and your shepherd's rod makes me feel safe."

Psalm 23:4

Saying goodbye

It's hard when people go away
When they go and can't just stay
Sometimes gone for just a while
But sometimes it is longer

They were here, but now they're not
It makes me sad, I don't know what
To do without my special friends
But I know I can remember

Their big smile, our happy faces
The fun we had in many places
Help us, God, to say goodbye
And know we find peace in you.

"God's home is now with his people. He will live with them, and they will be his own. Yes, God will make his home among his people. He will wipe all tears from their eyes, and there will be no more death, suffering, crying, or pain. These things of the past are gone forever."

Revelation 21:3,4

A prayer for peace

Jesus, you see all the fighting in our world,

You see all our shouting and arguing.

Help us to learn how to love each other

Just like you love us.

Please will you help the people in

....

To stop fighting and find a way
to live together happily.

Please help, Jesus.

You are the Prince of Peace.

"A child has been born for us. We have been given a son who will be our ruler. His names will be Wonderful Advisor and Mighty God, Eternal Father and Prince of Peace."

Isaiah 9:6

A prayer for people in need

Not all people have a home
Or a place to call their own
Jesus, please help those with none
To find a place where they belong
When they're hungry, give them food
When they're sad, please lift their mood
When they're scared, please keep them safe
If they lose hope, please give them faith.

"So whenever we are in need, we should come bravely before the throne of our merciful God. There we will be treated with undeserved kindness, and we will find help."

Hebrews 4:16

A prayer about change

When things change it's sometimes hard
To stop my worries winning
What will happen, when and where?
My head seems to be spinning
Other people struggle too
If too many things are new
Help us all to calmly trust
That you are always there with us.

"Jesus Christ never changes! He is the same yesterday, today, and forever."

Hebrews 13:8

Ask a grown-up to help you write down the names of all the people you want to pray for...

Children and adults alike love our Bible Friends books and resources. They're perfect as gifts, and for use at home, school and in groups for early-years children.

The Big Bible Activity Book

978 1 78506 557 6

£11.99

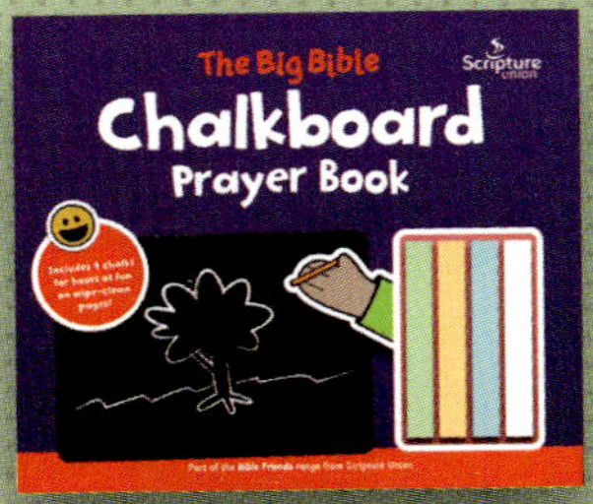

The Big Bible Chalkboard Prayer Book

978 1 78506 571 2

£7.99

The Big Bible Bookmarks

978 1 78506 561 3

£2.99

(2 designs in pack of 10)

The Big Bible Storybook

Hardback: 978 1 84427 228 0

£13.99

Paperback: 978 1 78506 190 5

£9.99

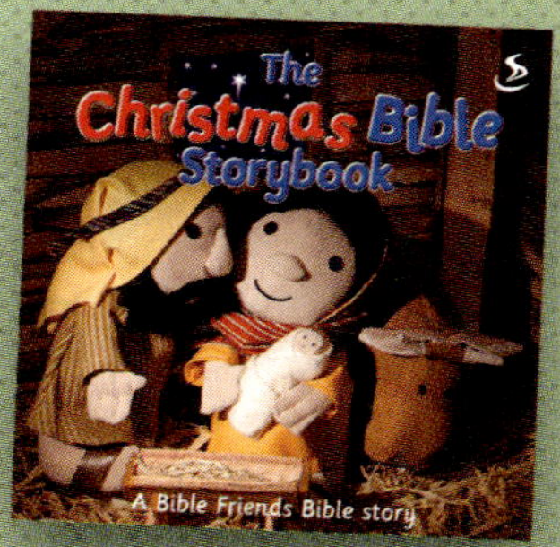

The Christmas Bible Storybook

978 1 84427 291 4

£3.99

The Easter Bible Storybook

978 1 84427 292 1

£3.99

To see the complete range and to order go to **www.scriptureunion.org.uk/Biblefriends**